STITCH IT FOR
Fall

Lynette Anderson

D&C
David and Charles
www.stitchcraftcreate.co.uk

Contents

Introduction

Creating the warm and welcoming projects in this book is the ideal way to celebrate autumn, and cope with chilly mornings and misty days. Take some time for yourself and sew as you watch the foliage turn to glorious shades of red and gold, the fruit ripen on the trees and the birds enjoy the bountiful harvest of seeds.

I've had such fun creating the projects for this book using my fabric collection called 'Mending Fences'. I love texture and depth and like to combine appliqué, hand embroidery and simple piecing in my projects. Growing up in the country has given me such fond memories. I loved riding horses and went to one of the village farms, where the horses needed exercise. The first pony I ever rode, called Misty, was sweet tempered and an ideal pony to learn on. As I grew taller, Gertie, a large hunter, became my favourite horse. I still have a horseshoe from each of these lovely animals. Whenever I see them among my childhood treasures they evoke memories of a time when life was slower and filled with adventures.

The wide ranging projects presented in this book are sure to adorn your home beautifully or make fabulous gifts to give to family and friends. Prepare for cooler days with the lovely Farmyard in Fall Quilt, with its rustic prints and cosy shades. Surprise a friend with the gift of the fun Mother Hen Tea Cosy, complete with three-dimensional fabric feathers. Cheerful sunflowers are perfect for decorating the useful Sunflower Purse. Plump hens feature on an easy-to-make Chicken Table Centre in mellow seasonal colours and patchwork squares and strips. If you love hand sewing the Apple Tree Farm Picture is perfect to capture the joys of autumn. A Striped Tote Bag in pale golds, pinks and reds of the season is great for shopping. A charming seasonal scene created in a punchneedle design can decorate any wicker basket, as the delightful Mrs Hen Basket shows. An enchanting mixture of stitchery, appliqué and Ohio Star patchwork captures the many pleasures of the season in the Sunflower Paddock Pillow.

All techniques are clearly described and templates are given full size to make creating these pieces easy and enjoyable. I hope that you relish the pleasures that autumn has to offer as you stitch these lovely projects.

Dedication
To my brother Andrew, who joined me in all my childhood adventures
and who always took the blame when we got home late for dinner!

General Techniques

This section describes the basic techniques you will need to make and finish off the projects in this book, from transferring designs to binding a finished quilt. Beginners should find it very useful.

Sewing and Pressing

Patchwork or pieced work requires accurate seams. For really accurate piecing sew a bare ¼in (6mm) seam, as this will allow for thread thickness and the tiny amount of fabric taken up when the seam is pressed.

Generally, press seams towards the darker fabric to avoid dark colours showing through on the right side. Press joining seams in opposite directions so they lock together and make the flattest join. Press (don't iron) and be careful with steam as this can stretch fabric.

Joining Strips

Sometimes fabric strips need to be joined together for borders or binding. Joining them with a diagonal seam at a 45-degree angle will make them less noticeable, as will pressing the seams open (Fig 1).

Fig 1

A   B

Making Bias Binding

Bias binding is made from fabric strips cut on the cross grain (bias) direction of the fabric, which makes the strips more flexible.

one Fold the fabric in half diagonally and crease lightly. Open out and cut strips 1¼in (3.2cm) wide diagonally across the fabric. Join the strips to the length required.

two Fold and press about ¼in (6mm) of fabric towards the wrong side along the entire length.

Using Templates

The project templates are given full size in the Template section. Trace the template on to paper or thin card, cut out and use as a pattern to cut the shape from paper. Before cutting out check whether a ¼in (6mm) seam allowance is needed, which it will be if using a needle-turn appliqué technique.

Reversing templates

Templates being used for fusible web appliqué will need to be reversed (flipped), but not if the design is symmetrical. You could place a copy of the template on to a light source with the template right side down rather than up and trace it this way. You could also trace the template on to tracing paper, turn the tracing paper over and trace the template again on to paper.

Transferring Designs

Designs can be transferred on to fabric in various ways. I use a light source, such as a light box, a window or a light under a glass table. Iron your fabric so it is free of creases. Place the design right side up and then the fabric right side up on top, taping it in place. Use a fine-tipped fabric marking pen or a pencil to trace the design. If the marks might show later then use an erasable marker, such as an air-erasable or water-soluble one.

English Paper Piecing

This type of patchwork is also called English patchwork and uses templates, usually made of paper or thin card. Fabric pieces are wrapped around the template and tacked (basted) to it. The patches are then hand sewn together and the papers removed. You could use pre-cut water-soluble hexagons – see the Striped Tote Bag.

one From a master template, create enough paper templates for the project. When cutting out the fabric pieces you need to allow for a ¼in (6mm) seam all round. Make one master template but this time add a ¼in (6mm) seam allowance all round and use this to cut out your fabric pieces.

two Follow Figs 2A–D and pin a paper template to a fabric shape and fold the seam allowance over the edges of the template, tacking (basting) in place through all layers. Keep the fabric firm around the paper shape and tuck in all points neatly. Repeat with all the fabric pieces.

three Place two fabric shapes right sides together, aligning edges and use small whip stitches to sew them together through the folded fabric but not through the paper (Fig 2E). Place a third fabric shape right sides together with the second and sew together. Continue building the design in this way. Once all stitching is finished remove the tacking and the papers.

Fig 2

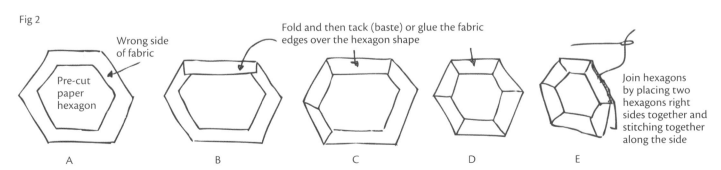

Wrong side of fabric

Pre-cut paper hexagon

Fold and then tack (baste) or glue the fabric edges over the hexagon shape

Join hexagons by placing two hexagons right sides together and stitching together along the side

A   B   C   D   E

Appliqué Methods

Appliqué is the technique of fixing one fabric shape or pattern on top of another, and can be done in various ways. I normally use two methods for my projects – needle-turn appliqué and fusible web appliqué. You may also like to use an appliqué mat.

Needle-turn method

This is a traditional method of hand appliqué where each appliqué piece has a seam turned under all round and is stitched into position on the background fabric. The appliqué shapes may be drawn freehand or templates used, as I have done for the designs in this book.

one   Mark the appliqué shape on the right side of your fabric and then mark another line further out all round for the seam allowance. This is usually ¼in (6mm) but may change depending on the size of the appliqué piece being stitched and type of fabric being used. Smaller pieces may only need a ⅛in (3mm) allowance to reduce bulk. Clip the seam allowance on concave curves (the inward ones) to make it easier to turn the seam under.

two   For each appliqué piece turn the seam allowance under all round and press. Position the appliqué on the background fabric and stitch into place with tiny slip stitches all round. Press when finished. Some people like to use the needle to turn the seam under as they stitch the appliqué in place. Press the finished appliqués.

Fusible web method

Fusible web has an adhesive that melts when heated so when the web is placed between two fabrics the heat of an iron causes the fabrics to fuse together, which makes it ideal for appliqué.

one   When using templates for fusible web appliqué they need to be flipped or reversed because you will be drawing the shape on the back of the fabric – see Reversing Templates. Trace around each template on to the paper side of the fusible web, leaving about ½in (1.3cm) around each shape. Cut out roughly around

each shape. Iron the fusible web, paper side up, on to the wrong side of the appliqué fabric and then cut out accurately on your drawn line.

two   When the fusible web is cool, peel off the backing paper and place the appliqué in position on your project, right side up. (Check with the template to see which pieces need to go under other pieces, shown by dotted lines on the pattern.) Fuse into place with a medium-hot iron for about ten seconds. Allow the appliqué to cool.

three   The edge of the appliqué can be secured further by stitches. I normally use blanket stitch as I like the hand-crafted look but machine satin stitch can also be used.

Making a Quilt Sandwich

A quilt sandwich is a term often used to describe the three layers of a quilt – the top, the wadding (batting) and the backing.

one   Press your backing fabric and hang out your wadding to reduce creases. Cut out your wadding and backing about 4in (10.2cm) larger all round than the quilt top. Prepare the quilt top by cutting off or tying in stray ends, pressing it and pressing seam allowances so they lay as flat as possible.

two   Lay the backing fabric right side down on a flat surface and tape the corners to keep it flat. Put the wadding on top, smoothing out wrinkles. Now put the quilt top right side up on top.

three   Secure the three layers together by using pins or safety pins, tacking (basting) or spray glue. If using pins or tacking, use a grid pattern spacing the lines out about 3in–6in (7.6cm–15.2cm) apart. The sandwich is now ready for quilting.

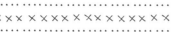 

Quilting

Quilting adds texture and interest to a quilt and secures all the layers together. I have used a combination of hand and machine quilting on the projects in this book. When starting and finishing hand or machine quilting, the starting knot and the thread end need to be hidden in the wadding (batting).

If you need to mark a quilting design on your top this can be done before or after you have made the quilt sandwich. There are many marking pens and pencils available but test them on scrap fabric first. If you are machine quilting, marking lines are more easily covered up. For hand quilting you might prefer to use a removable marker or a light pencil. Some water-erasable markers are set by the heat of an iron so take care when pressing the work.

Binding

Binding a quilt creates a neat and secure edge. A double-fold binding is more durable than a single-fold one.

one   Measure your completed quilt top around all edges and add about 8in (20.3cm) extra. Cut 2½in (6.3cm) wide strips and join them all together to make the length needed. Fold the binding in half along the length and press.

two   Start midway along one side of the quilt and pin the binding along the edge, aligning raw edges. Stitch the binding to the quilt through all layers using a ¼in (6mm) seam until you reach a corner when you should stop ¼in (6mm) away from the end (Fig 3A).

three   Remove the work from the machine and fold the binding up, northwards, so it is aligned straight with the edge of the quilt (Fig 3B).

four   Hold the corner and fold the binding back down, southwards, aligning it with the raw edge and with the folded corner square. Pin in position and begin sewing again, from the top and over the fold, continuing down the next edge (Fig 3C). Repeat with the other corners of the quilt.

five   When you are nearing the starting point stop 6in (15.2cm) away. Fold back the beginning and end of the binding, so they touch and mark these folds with a pin. Cut the binding ¼in (6mm) from the pin, open out the binding and join with a ¼in (6mm) seam. Press the seam open, re-fold it and slipstitch in place.

six   Now fold the binding over to the back of the quilt and slipstitch it in place. Fold the mitres at the corner neatly and secure with tiny slipstitches.

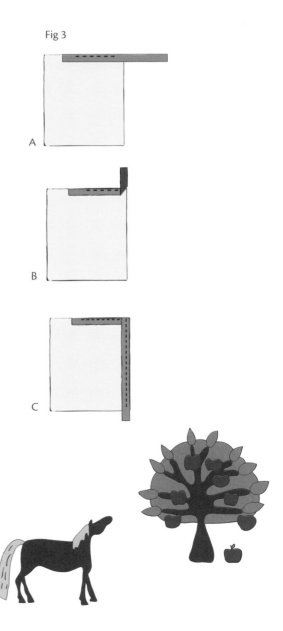

Fig 3

A

B

C

7

Embroidery Stitches

I have used various stitches to create the stitcheries on the projects in this book. I used Cosmo stranded embroidery threads but DMC equivalents are given here. The stitches are all easy to work and fun to do – just follow the simple diagrams.

Embroidery Threads

The projects in this book use Cosmo stranded embroidery threads but DMC alternatives have been provided here.

Cosmo code	Colour	DMC code
236	dusky pink	3726
245	red	815
312	dark brown	838
364	cream	712
368	light brown	3790
385	brown	839
575	gold	3829
734	blue	930
763	light mauve	3041
895	charcoal	844
924	light green	3012
925	green	3011
982	faded blue	3768

Backstitch

Backstitch is an outlining stitch that I also use to 'draw' parts of the design. It is really easy to work and can follow any parts of a design you choose.

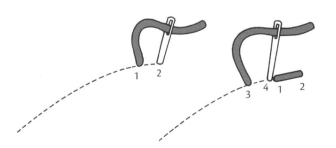

Blanket stitch

Blanket stitch can be used to edge appliqué motifs and stitched in a circle for flowers. Start at the edge of the appliqué shape, taking the needle through from the back of work and up to the front of the shape that you are appliquéing a small distance in from the edge where you started (A). Pull the thread through to form a loop (B). Put your needle through the loop from front to back, making sure the loop is not twisted. As you pull the thread into place lift the stitch slightly so that it sits on top of the raw edge rather than sliding underneath (C). Pull the thread firmly into place to avoid loose, floppy stitches. Continue on to make the next stitch (D).

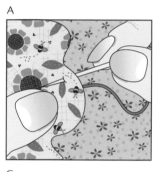 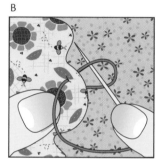

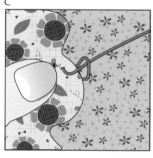 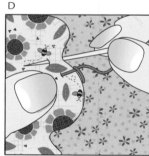

Chain stitch

This stitch can be worked in straight or curved lines for stems and as a single detached stitch.

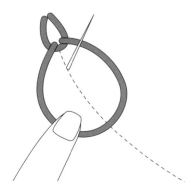

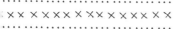 

Cross stitch

A simple cross stitch can be used to add pattern to stitcheries, particularly on animal coats.

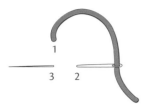 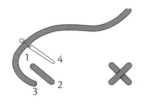

Herringbone stitch

This embroidery stitch is used as a decorative stitch and can also be used as a joining stitch.

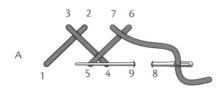

French knot

These little knots are easy to form and are useful for eyes and other details.

  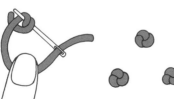

Lazy daisy stitch

This decorative stitch is great for flowers especially if the stitches are worked in a circle.

Long stitch

Long stitch is just a single long stitch. It is useful for coat markings, cat's whiskers and so on.

Running stitch

These are evenly spaced stitches that can run in any direction or pattern you choose. Quilting stitch is a running stitch.

Satin stitch

This stitch is used to fill in areas of a design with long stitches worked side by side.

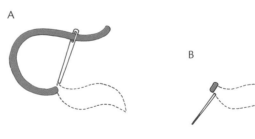

Farmyard in Fall Quilt

This gorgeous throw-sized quilt is fun to make and will look great on the back of your sofa. Using a variety of fabrics in coordinated rustic prints and patterns in mellow autumn colours creates a visual treat and is the perfect way to use up all your leftover fabric scraps.

Finished size: 52in x 58in (132cm x 147cm) approximately.

What You Will Need

* ¼yd/m each of seven coordinating fabrics for pieced blocks

* ⅜yd/m each of seven coordinating fabrics for pieced blocks

* ¼yd/m of blue print for inner border

* ⅓yd/m of cream floral print for middle border

* ⅝yd/m of dusky pink print for outer border

* Wadding (batting) 56in x 62in (142cm x 158cm) approximately

* Backing fabric 56in x 62in (142cm x 158cm) approximately

* Suitable sewing and quilting threads

* Fine-tipped fabric marking pen

Cutting the Squares

one From each of the seven ¼yd/m coordinating fabrics for the pieced blocks, cut two 42in x 3½in (106.7cm x 8.9cm) strips. From these cut sixteen 3½in (8.9cm) squares. From each of the seven ⅜yd/m coordinating fabrics for the pieced blocks cut two 6½in x 42in (16.5cm x 106.7cm) strips and from these cut eight 6½in (16.5cm) squares.

Making the Blocks

two Select two 3½in (8.9cm) matching squares and one coordinating 6½in (16.5cm) square. On the wrong side of the fabric use a fine-tipped fabric pen to draw a diagonal line on one of the 3½in (8.9cm) squares (Fig 1A). Place it right sides together on one corner of the 6½in (16.5cm) square and stitch on the drawn line. Trim ¼in (6mm) away from the sewn line then open and press (Fig 1B). Repeat with the other 3½in (8.9cm) square on the opposite diagonal corner of the same 6½in (16.5cm) square to complete one block (Fig 1C). Make a total of eight blocks using the same colourway and press.

three From the remaining 3½in (8.9cm) and 6½in (16.5cm) squares, follow the step 2 instructions to make another six sets of eight blocks. You will now have fifty-six blocks in total.

Fig 1

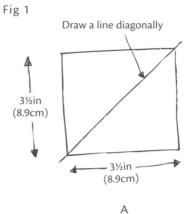

Draw a line diagonally

3½in (8.9cm)

3½in (8.9cm)

A

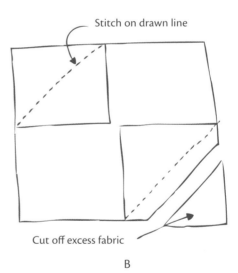

Stitch on drawn line

Cut off excess fabric

B

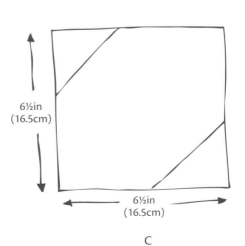

6½in (16.5cm)

6½in (16.5cm)

C

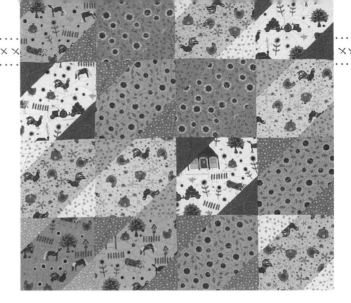

Joining the Blocks

four To assemble the rows, arrange one block from each colourway in a row of seven blocks in total and sew together as shown in Fig 2, matching seams carefully. Press the seams. Repeat for the remaining blocks, making sure that you arrange the colour blocks in each row in a different order to form an attractive pattern. Now sew the rows together, matching seams. Press the quilt top.

Fig 2

Adding the Inner Border

five From the blue print inner border fabric, cut five strips each 1in x 42in (2.5cm x 106.7cm) and piece strips using diagonal seams to create a long length. From this cut two 1in x 48½in (2.5cm x 123.2cm) strips for the side borders and cut two 1in x 43½in (2.5cm x 110.5cm) strips for the top and bottom borders. Join the side borders to the quilt first at opposite sides and press seams. Next sew on the top and bottom borders and press seams.

six From the cream floral print inner border fabric cut five 2in x 42in (5cm x 106.7cm) strips and piece strips using diagonal seams to create a long length. From this cut two 2in x 49½in (5cm x 125.7cm) strips for the side borders and cut two 2in x 46½in (2cm x 118cm) strips for the top and bottom borders. Join the side borders to the quilt first at opposite sides and press seams. Next sew on the top and bottom borders and press seams again.

Adding the Outer Border

seven From the outer border fabric cut six 3½in x 42in (8.9cm x 106.7cm) strips and piece strips using diagonal seams to create a long length. From this cut four 3½in x 52½in (8.9cm x 133.4cm) strips. Join two of the outer border strips to the opposite long sides of the quilt centre and press seams. Next sew two outer border strips to the remaining opposite short sides of the quilt centre to complete the quilt top.

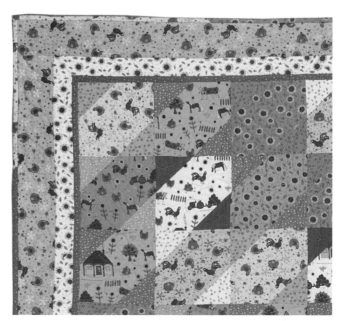

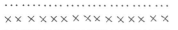

Quilting

eight Prepare the quilt for quilting using your wadding (batting) and backing fabric. Quilt as desired. See General Techniques: Quilting.

Binding the Quilt

nine Using the remaining fabric scraps make binding about 230in (585cm) long. Bind the quilt using your preferred method. See General Techniques: Binding.

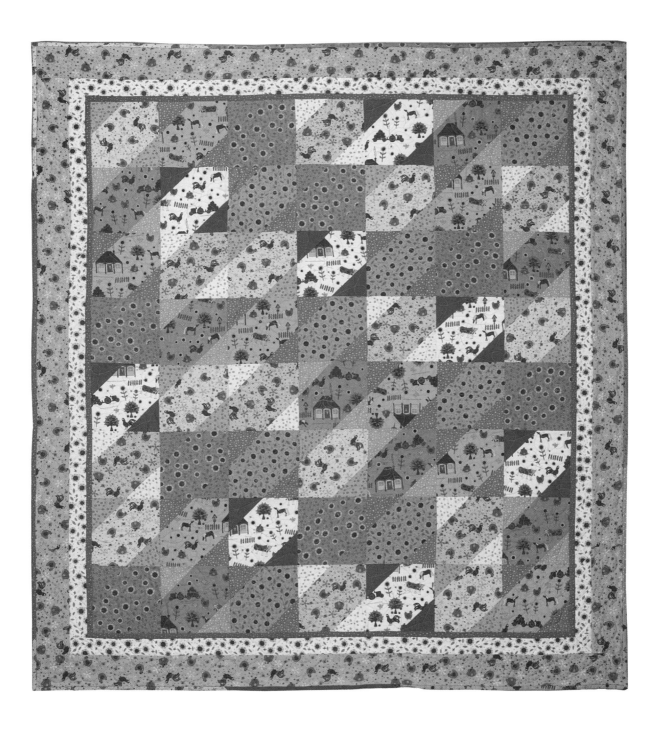

Mother Hen Tea Cosy

I have fond childhood memories of my mother's charming hen tea cosy with its loose fabric feathers and beady button eyes. I hope I have captured the fun character of that cosy here with my own delightful feathered friend to brighten up your kitchen.

Finished size: 10½in x 14in (26.7cm x 35.5cm) approximately.

What You Will Need

* 12in (30.5cm) x width of fabric of beige yarn dye for hen body

* 12in (30.5cm) x width of fabric of blue print for lining

* 4in x 18in (10.2cm x 45.7cm) each of twelve assorted fabrics for feathers

* 10½in x 36in (26.7cm x 91.5cm) of lightweight iron-on pellon for feathers

* 12in (30.5cm) x width of fabric of firm fusible wadding (batting) for hen body (I used Inn-Control Plus™ – see Suppliers)

* 2in x 4in (5cm x 10.2cm) of red wool for hen's wattle and comb

* 2in (5cm) square of gold wool for beak

* Two buttons ¾in (1.9cm) diameter for eyes (I used vintage buttons)

* 3in x 4in (7.6cm x 10.2cm) of template plastic

* Fabric pen

Cutting the Pieces

one   Use the templates provided to make a paper template for the hen's body. Use the paper template to cut out two body parts in beige yarn dye fabric and two in blue print lining fabric, adding seam allowances. Cut two in firm fusible wadding (batting), this time without seam allowance on the bottom edge of the hen.

Making the Fabric Feathers

two   Use the feather template provided to cut a template from template plastic. Take the twelve assorted 4in x 18in (10.2cm x 45.7cm) fabrics and with right sides together, fold each piece in half lengthwise and cut on the fold (Fig 1A–B).

three   Fold and press approximately ½in (1.3cm) of the top of each fabric length to the wrong side. Then with right sides together make sure that the folded edge on both pieces of the feather is lined up (Fig 2A). Cut the lightweight iron-on pellon into 3½in (8.9cm) strips and bond to the wrong side of one of each pairs of fabric (do not apply the pellon over the turn back) (Fig 2B).

Fig 2

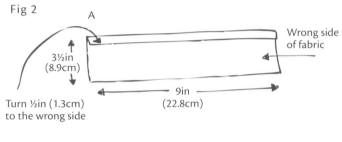

four   On the opposite side to where you have fused the pellon and using a suitable marking pen, trace around the plastic feather template leaving approximately ½in (1.3cm) between each fabric feather for the seam allowance (Fig 3A). Stitch on the drawn line, then cut out ¼in (6mm) beyond the drawn line (Fig 3B). Turn to the right side and press. Repeat to make a total of thirty-five fabric feathers.

Fig 1

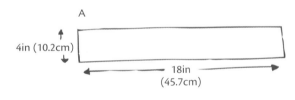

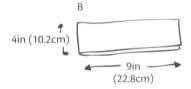

Fig 3

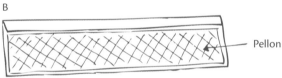

Attaching the Feathers

five   Using the body template as a guide, draw on the positioning lines for the fabric feathers with a suitable marking pen. Starting with row A, position and pin four of the feathers in place. Each fabric feather will need a small tuck in the centre to create some shape and to allow them to fit in the allocated space (Fig 4A). Machine stitch the fabric feathers in place (Fig 4B). Continue adding rows of feathers in the same way and press. Repeat for the other side of the hen and press.

six   Using the template as a guide for positioning, pin and stitch three fabric tail feathers in position between E and F, facing the feathers inwards. Use the templates provided to cut the wattle and comb from red wool and the beak from gold wool. Position and stitch in place between G and H on the hen's body (Fig 5).

Fig 5

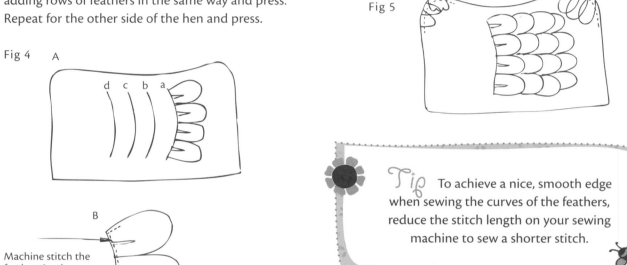

Fig 4   A

d c b a

B

Machine stitch the
feathers in place

Tip   To achieve a nice, smooth edge when sewing the curves of the feathers, reduce the stitch length on your sewing machine to sew a shorter stitch.

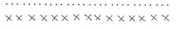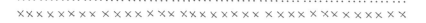

Assembling the Tea Cosy

seven   Layer the hen together as shown in Fig 6, using the body shapes cut from beige yarn dye fabric, blue print lining fabric and fusible wadding (batting) in step 1.

eight   Stitch the layers together, leaving the bottom edge open (Fig 7). Now turn the hen to the right side and slip stitch the lining in place. Finally, attach the two buttons in place for the hen's eyes by stitching through all the layers. Gently press the finished work. Time for a cup of tea!

Fig 6

Firm wadding (batting)
Lining
Firm wadding (batting)
Yarn dye outer

Fig 7

Stitch together

Leave open

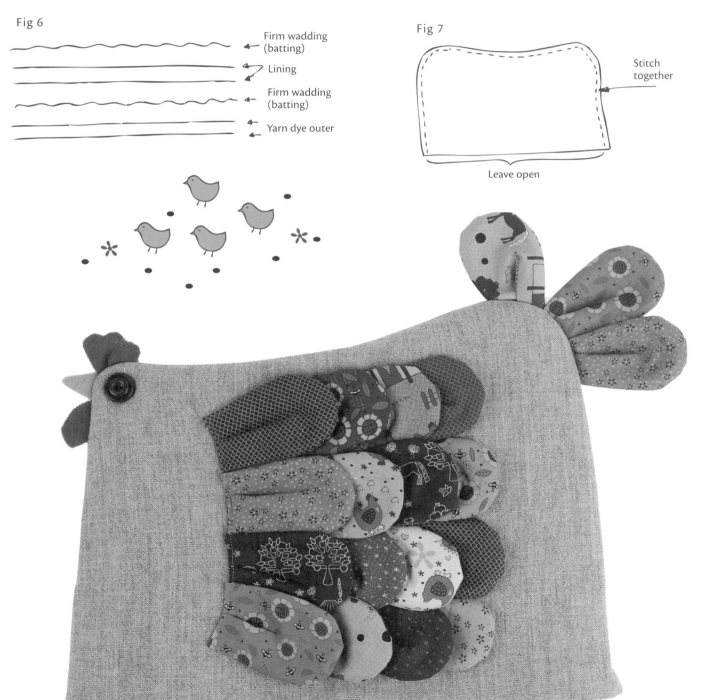

Sunflower Purse

This charming little purse combines stitchery with appliqué to create a sweet scene of a hen tempted by sunflowers ripe with seed on a grassy hill. It is the perfect place to store all your spare change.

Finished size: 4¼in x 2½in (10.8cm x 6.4cm) approximately.

What You Will Need

* 6in (15.2cm) square of cream print for background
* 6in (15.2cm) square of pink floral print for back of purse
* 8in x 6in (20.3cm x 15.2cm) of print lining fabric
* 11in (28cm) square of brown print for bias binding and sunflower centres
* 1½in x 6in (3.8cm x 15.2cm) of green print for grass
* 2in (5cm) square of light brown print for chick
* 1in (2.5cm) square of pale pink print for wing
* 1in x 2in (2.5cm x 5cm) of gold wool for sunflower petals
* Antique gold zip (zipper) 5in (12.7cm) long

* 6in (15.2cm) square of stitchery stabilizer (optional)
* 8in x 6in (20.3cm x 15.2cm) of lightweight iron-on pellon
* Cosmo stranded embroidery thread: 368 pale brown, 982 faded blue, 895 charcoal, 245 red and 924 light green (see General Techniques: Embroidery Threads for DMC alternatives)
* Fine-tipped fabric marking pen
* Masking tape ½in (1.3cm) wide
* Template plastic
* Roxanne's Glue Baste It ™ (optional)

Making the Bias Binding

one From brown print make 20in (51cm) of bias binding – see Making Bias Binding. Put aside for later.

Transferring the Stitchery Design

two Using the template and light source, centre the cream background fabric right side up on the pattern. Use a fabric pen to trace the stitchery. If using iron-on stabilizer, iron it on before working the stitchery.

Working the Appliqué

three Using the templates and your favourite method of appliqué, apply the hill, hen and wing. If using needle-turn appliqué, add seam allowances to the shapes. Stitch the appliqués in position with blind hem stitch and thread matching the background fabric. Press the finished appliqués. Using a fine fabric pen, transfer the surface stitchery lines for the heart freehand or using a light box. Cut two sunflowers from gold wool and sew in place with the flower centres.

Working the Stitchery

four The stitches used are backstitch (BS), satin stitch (SS), running stitch (RS) and French knots (FK). Code numbers are for Cosmo stranded embroidery threads but you could use DMC alternatives. Use two strands and gently press when stitching is complete.

Making Up the Purse

five From template plastic make templates A and B (seam allowances are included). Trace template A onto the cream fabric. Cut out on the line. Trace template B on the pink print. Cut out on the line. Sew A and B right sides together along the straight edge (Fig 1).

Fig 1

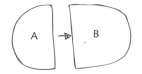

six Bond pellon to the wrong side of the lining fabric. Put the stitched purse outer right side up on the pellon and machine quilt a diagonal grid pattern (Fig 2).

Key for Threads and Stitches

Cosmo 368 pale brown
Sunflower stems (BS)

Cosmo 982 faded blue
Dots in sky (FK)

Cosmo 895 charcoal
Hen's legs (BS)
Hen's beak (SS)
Hen's eye (FK)

Cosmo 245 red
Hen's heart (SS)
Hen's comb and wattle (SS)

Cosmo 924 light green
Leaves (BS)
Leaf veins (RS)

Use the masking tape as a guide, quilting either side of the tape and moving it across the fabric. Trim pellon and lining to the same size as the stitched purse outer.

Fig 2

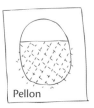

Pellon

seven Bind the edge of the oval. With right sides together and matching the top curve of the purse, check the zip length and pin mark where it starts and stops (Fig 3). Hand stitch the side of the purse together. Repeat for other side. Backstitch the zip into place, first on one side, then the other (Fig 4). To neaten the inside, stitch the selvedge side of the zip to the purse lining. To make a flat bottom, fold and machine stitch across the corner on both sides (Fig 5). Turn through to the right side.

Fig 3

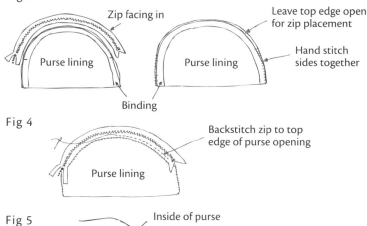

Zip facing in

Leave top edge open for zip placement

Purse lining

Purse lining

Hand stitch sides together

Binding

Fig 4

Backstitch zip to top edge of purse opening

Purse lining

Fig 5

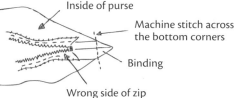

Inside of purse

Machine stitch across the bottom corners

Binding

Wrong side of zip

Chicken Table Centre

Any table or sideboard would look wonderful topped with this fun hen centrepiece. I have tried to capture the allure of the autumn season by combining simple piecing and easy appliqué techniques with charming prints and rustic colourways.

Finished size: 24in (61cm) square approximately.

What You Will Need

* 14in (35.6cm) square of yarn dye fabric for centre triangles and corner squares

* 5in x 20in (12.7cm x 50.8cm) of brown check print for hens

* 2in x 12in (5cm x 30.5cm) of light brown print for wings

* 2in x 8in (5cm x 20.3cm) of red print for combs, wattles and beaks

* 4in (10.2cm) wide strip x width of fabric each of six coordinating print fabrics for centre and border

* 8in (30.3cm) wide strip x width of fabric of binding fabric

* Wadding (batting) 28in (71cm) square

* Backing fabric 28in (71cm) square

* BSuitable sewing and quilting threads

* Four small buttons in brown for eyes

* Roxanne's Glue Baste It ™ (optional)

* Fabric marking pen

Cutting the Squares for the Centre

one From the six coordinating print fabrics, cut one 2½in (6.4cm) wide strip x width of fabric. Cross cut six 2½in (6.4in) squares from each fabric. Cut twelve 1½in x 3½in (3.8cm x 8.9cm) strips from the remainder of each fabric. From the yarn dye fabric, cut two 9⅜in (24cm) squares. Using a suitable fabric marking pen, draw a diagonal line across these squares and cut to make four corner triangles (Fig 1).

Fig 1

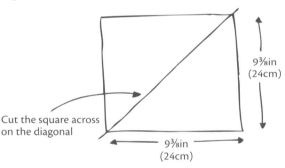

Cut the square across on the diagonal

9⅜in (24cm)

9⅜in (24cm)

Working the Appliqué

two Using the templates provided and your favourite method of appliqué (see General Techniques: Appliqué Methods), apply the hens to the large corner triangles. If using needle-turn appliqué (as I did) you will need to add seam allowances to the shapes. I made paper templates for the appliqué shapes, drew around the templates onto the wrong side of my chosen fabrics, added a small seam allowance and cut the pieces out. Turn the seam allowance under all round.

three Stitch the appliqué shapes in position using a blind hem stitch and thread that matches the background fabric so it doesn't show. Press the finished appliqués on the wrong side and then on the right side.

Tip I like to use Roxanne's Glue Baste It to fix the appliqué shapes in position on the background. You could use pins but I don't like the way the thread always gets caught around pins. Being a soccer mum, I love to take my sewing whilst I watch the boys training and I never used to know what to do with the pins when I took them out. Using glue means the problem is solved!

Making the Centre Square

four Arrange the 2½in (6.4cm) squares in six rows of six in a pleasing layout. Stitch together as shown in Fig 2, and then press.

five Join one appliquéd corner triangle to each side of the pieced centre and press (Fig 3).

Fig 2

Join the squares into rows

Join the rows together

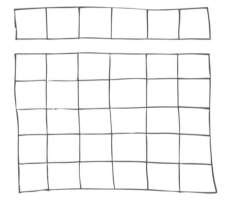

Adding the Border

six Join seventeen 1½in x 3½in (3.8cm x 8.9cm) strips together in a row. Repeat to make a second set and press. Join the strips to the two opposite sides of the table centre (Fig 4A), easing to fit.

seven Join seventeen 1½in x 3½in (3.8cm x 8.9cm) strips together as before, this time adding a 3½in (8.9cm) square of yarn dye fabric to each end of the rows. Repeat to make a second set and join these to the top and bottom of the table centre (Fig 4B).

Fig 4A

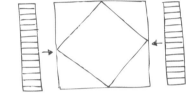

Fig 4B

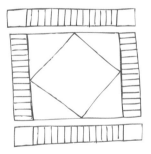

Fig 3

Sew on the appliquéd corner triangles

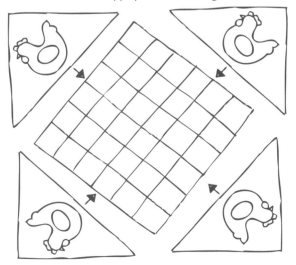

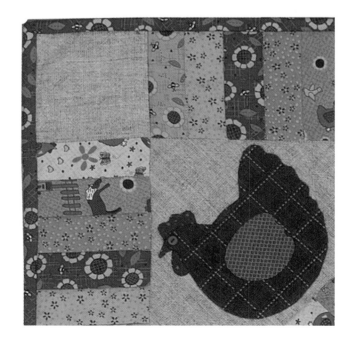

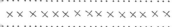

Quilting

eight Prepare for quilting by layering the backing, wadding (batting) and top. I did a cross hatch pattern in the centre pieced square and machine quilted in the ditch on the outer border. See General Techniques: Quilting.

Binding

nine Prepare the binding fabric and use your preferred method to attach the binding (see General Techniques: Binding). Stitch the buttons in place for the eyes to finish.

Apple Tree Farm Picture

It looks like the apples are ready to be harvested here at Apple Tree Farm. Free-range hens are roaming the paddocks while sunflowers, straight and tall, fill the fields. A combination of appliqué and stitchery with wool sunflowers and lovely hand-painted buttons create a lovely scene to adorn your wall.

Finished size: 6in (15.2cm) diameter approximately.

What You Will Need

* 10in (26.4cm) square of cream checked yarn dye for background

* 4in x 5in (10.2cm x 12.7cm) of cream-on-cream plaid for hill

* 3in x 6½in (7.6cm x 16.5cm) of cream/beige plaid for hill

* 2in x 3in (5cm x 7.6cm) of light brown print for house

* 2in (5cm) square of dark red print for roof

* 1in (2.5cm) square of dark blue print for door

* 2in (5cm) square of gold wool for sunflowers

* 2in (5cm) square of brown print for sunflower centres

* 10in (25cm) square of stitchery stabilizer (optional)

* 8in (20.3cm) square of cotton wadding (batting)

* Cosmo stranded embroidery threads: 236 dusky pink, 245 red, 312 dark brown, 364 cream, 385 brown, 575 gold, 895 charcoal, 925 dark green and 982 faded blue

* Three sunflower buttons

* Fine-tipped fabric marking pen

* Hot glue gun with glue

* Roxanne's Glue Baste It ™ (optional)

* Round wooden frame to fit (ideally with removable insert at the back)

Transferring the Design

one   Use the templates provided. Using a light source such as a light box or a window, place the cream checked background fabric right side up and centrally over the stitchery design and trace the design using a fine-tipped fabric marking pen.

two   If using an iron-on stitchery stabilizer, iron it on before starting the stitching to avoid thread shadows showing on the front of the work. Place the shiny side of the stabilizer on to the wrong side of your fabric and follow the manufacturer's instructions to bond in place.

Working the Appliqué

three   You can do the appliqué before or after the stitchery has been completed – I do mine before. Using your favourite method of appliqué, apply the hills, house, roofs and door. If using needle-turn appliqué (as I did) you will need to add seam allowance to the shapes. I made paper templates for the appliqué shapes and drew around the templates onto the wrong side of my chosen fabrics. I cut the pieces out, added a small seam allowance and turned the seam allowance under all round. Once the edges are turned under and tacked (basted), press the shapes, first on the wrong side and then on the right side. I like to use Roxanne's Glue Baste It ™ to fix the shapes in position on the background, although you can use pins.

four   Stitch the appliqué shapes in position using a blind hem stitch and thread that matches the background fabric so it doesn't show.

Transferring the Stitchery Design

five   Using a fine-tipped fabric marking pen transfer the surface stitchery lines for the tree roots, fallen apple, windows, hens, and sunflower stems and leaves either freehand or using a light box.

Tip If you are unable to see though your background fabric to trace the design, try drawing over the pattern lines with a thicker felt tip pen. This will make it show more clearly through the fabric.

Working the Stitchery

six   Now work the stitchery. The stitches used are backstitch (BS), satin stitch (SS), cross stitch (CS), running stitch (RS), lazy daisy (LD) and French knots (FK). Code numbers are for Cosmo stranded embroidery threads but you could use DMC alternatives (see General Techniques: Embroidery Threads). Use two strands unless otherwise stated. Gently press the piece when stitching is complete.

25

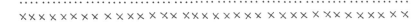

Key for Threads and Stitches

Cosmo 236 dusky pink
Apples on tree (SS)
Flower dots in field (FK)

Cosmo 245 red
Hens' wattles and combs (SS)
Heart hanging from string in tree (SS)

Cosmo 312 dark brown
Tree trunk and branches (BS)
Sunflower stems (BS)
Fence posts (BS)

Cosmo 364 cream
Smoke from chimney (BS)

Cosmo 385 light brown
Hens (BS)
Chimney (BS)
Fence wire, single strand (BS and CS)

Cosmo 575 gold
Hens' beaks (SS)
Hens' legs (BS)

Cosmo 895 charcoal
Hens' eyes (FK)
Crow on rooftop (BS)
Crow's legs (BS)
Crow's eye (FK)
Crow's beak (SS)

Window frames (BS)
Cross above door (CS)
String holding heart in tree (BS)

Cosmo 925 dark green
Leaves on tree (LD)
Sunflower leaves (BS)
Veins on sunflower leaves (RS)
Leaves in field (LD)
Hill lines (BS)
Dashed line under hill (RS)

Cosmo 982 faded blue
Dots in sky (FK)
Outer line (BS)

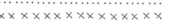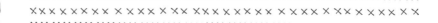

seven   Once all the stitching has been completed, gently press your work. Stitch the three sunflower buttons in place.

eight   Trim the design down, allowing sufficient excess fabric to suit your frame type. Cut a piece of cotton wadding (batting) to the same size as the wooden insert from your frame. Use a hot glue gun to glue the wadding to the wooden insert. I used a frame that had a removable insert at the back, making framing easy. Carefully centre the design over the wadding-covered insert and take the fabric over the edge of the insert to the back of the frame. Glue in place all round. Put into the frame and enjoy.

The picture really stands out in a natural wood frame. If you prefer, you could paint the frame in a colour that complements your fabrics and threads.

Striped Tote Bag

You can never have too many bags and this is a great one to add to your collection. The coordinating hexagons and stripes in shades of pink and brown make this tote too pretty to resist and the faux leather handles give it a really professional look!

Finished size: 12½in x 16in (31.8cm x 40.6cm) approximately.

What You Will Need

* Twelve 1⅞in x 14in (4.8cm x 35.5cm) strips from assorted prints

* Fifteen 4in (10.2cm) squares of assorted prints for hexagons

* 16½in (42cm) square of dusky pink floral print for back of bag

* Two 16½in (42cm) squares of brown print for lining

* Two 16½in (42cm) squares of firm fusible wadding (batting) (I used Inn-Control Plus™ – see Suppliers)

* Fifteen pre-cut water-soluble paper hexagons with 1½in (3.8cm) sides

* Fabric glue pen

* One pair of leather-look handles

* One clamp/pin holder – see Suppliers

* Template plastic

* Strong thread to match handles and suitable quilting threads

Making the Hexagon Patchwork

one Use the large hexagon template to make a template from template plastic (seam allowance included) and cut fifteen hexagons from the assorted coordinating prints. Centre a pre-cut water-soluble hexagon on the wrong side of the fabric and tack (baste) in place or use a glue pen – see General Techniques: English Paper Piecing. Repeat for all hexagons.

Tip You can make paper hexagons with 1½in (3.8cm) sides using the smaller template provided, however these will need to be taken off once the hexagons are joined. Water-soluble hexagons do not need to be removed.

two Stitch the hexagons together to form two rows (Fig 1) – see General Techniques: English Paper Piecing. Gently press the work.

Fig 1   Join the hexagons together in two rows

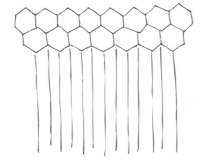

Joining the Strips

three Arrange the twelve assorted print strips in a pleasing arrangement, sew together using a ¼in (6mm) seam allowance and press. Place the joined rows of hexagons at the top of the joined strips and stitch in place (Fig 2).

Fig 2

Quilting the Bag

four Bond the fusible wadding (batting) to the wrong side of the front piece and also the 16½in (42cm) square for the back of the bag. Quilt as desired. Trim the bag front to 16½in (42cm) square.

Adding the Lining

five Put the two 16½in (42cm) squares of lining fabric right sides together and stitch around, leaving an opening on one side. To make corners at the bag base, machine stitch across the corner on both sides (Fig 3).

Fig 3

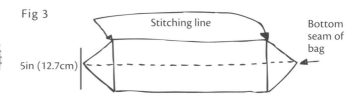

Stitching line

Bottom seam of bag

5in (12.7cm)

Assembling the Bag

six Place the bag front and back right sides together and matching side seams and stitch together, leaving the top open. Stitch the bag corners as you did for the lining.

seven With the bag right sides out, slip the lining over the top, right sides together and matching the top edges (Fig 4). Stitch around the top through all layers. Turn out through the opening in the lining. Machine stitch around the top of the bag, ¼in (6mm) from the top. Machine stitch the lining opening closed.

Fig 4

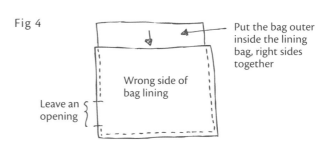

Put the bag outer inside the lining bag, right sides together

Wrong side of bag lining

Leave an opening

eight Sew the handles to the bag outer using a large backstitch and strong thread. If using handles with pre-punched holes, the clamp/pin holder will fix them while you are stitching. Time to go shopping!

Mrs Hen Basket

This charming little punchneedle design featuring Mrs Hen out on her morning walk is so simple and fun to make. Add it to any basket of your choosing to bring a smile to every shopping trip!

Finished design size: 5in x 3¼in (12.7cm x 8.2cm) approximately.

What You Will Need

* 12in (30cm) square of weaver's cloth

* Valdani variegated three-strand embroidery cotton (floss) spools: H212, 0154, P1, JP1, JP12, H204, H202, H205, P2 and P12 (see Suppliers)

* Cameo Ultra Punch tool (see Suppliers)

* Ric-rac braid 1yd/m

* Basket (I used one found in a secondhand/thrift shop)

* Hot glue gun with glue

* Fine-tipped fabric marking pen

* Light box (optional)

* 7in (17.8cm) embroidery hoop

Transferring the Punchneedle Design

one Take the square of weaver's cloth. Using the punchneedle design template and a light box or window, centre the cloth over the pattern. Use a fine-tipped fabric marking pen to transfer the pattern.

Tip You will notice that the punchneedle design has been drawn in reverse. This is correct, as you need to work from the back to the front of the design.

two Once the design has been transferred onto the cloth, place it into the embroidery hoop. Make sure that the fabric is tight in the hoop and that you do not distort the design as you tighten the fabric.

Punching the Design

three You are now ready to get punching! Follow the Cameo Ultra Punch instructions and the colour placement drawing. I used three strands of Valdani embroidery cotton throughout this project and the number one setting on the Cameo Ultra Punch needle. See Fig 1 for threading the needle and Fig 2 for the punching technique.

Fig 1

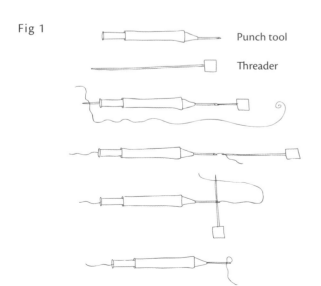

Punch tool

Threader

Fig 2

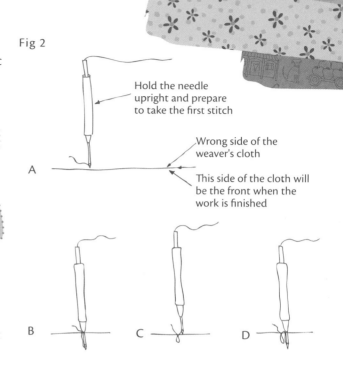

Hold the needle upright and prepare to take the first stitch

Wrong side of the weaver's cloth

This side of the cloth will be the front when the work is finished

A

B   C   D

Assembling the Basket

four Once you have finished punching your design, remove it from the embroidery hoop and gently press the cloth around the design. Leaving at least 1in (2.5cm) beyond the punchneedle, trim away the excess cloth. Turn the remaining cloth to the back of the punchneedle so you can't see it from the front and stitch it in place.

five Glue the ric-rac in place using the hot glue gun so that it shows just beyond the edge of the punched piece. Use the hot glue gun to glue the punchneedle piece to the front of your basket and enjoy!

Sunflower Paddock Pillow

Pillows are perfect for displaying stitchery and this one also has some pretty Ohio Star patchwork blocks. Happy in her retirement, Misty is enjoying her days grazing in the paddock. Misty was one of the first ponies I rode when I was a child; she was so sweet natured and I still have one of her horseshoes.

Finished size: 18in (45.7cm) square approximately.

What You Will Need

* 12in (30.5cm) square of cream print for stitchery background

* 8½in x 12½in (21.6cm x 31.8cm) of blue print for front panel

* 6in (15.2cm) square of brown print for horse and 3in (7.6cm) square of light brown print for mane and tail

* 3½in x 6in (8.9cm x 15.2cm) each of four assorted prints for Ohio Star backgrounds

* 2½in x 5in (6.4cm x 12.7cm) each of four assorted fabrics for Ohio Star points

* 2½in (6.4cm) square each of four prints for Ohio star inner triangles and 2in (5cm) square each of four assorted prints for star centre squares

* 1½in x 12½in (3.8cm x 31.8cm) of brown feature print

* 1in x 4in (4.5cm x 10.2cm) of brown print for sunflower centres

* 19in (48.3cm) x width of fabric of brown print for borders and pillow backing

* 5in (12.7cm) square of gold wool for sunflowers

* 5in (12.7cm) square of fusible web

* Two 18½in (47cm) squares of lightweight iron-on pellon

* Cosmo stranded embroidery threads: 982 faded blue, 312 dark brown, 575 gold, 924 light green, 895 charcoal and 925 dark green

* Stuffing for pillow

* Template plastic

Transferring the Design

one   Using the templates provided and a light source such as a light box or window, centre the stitchery background fabric right side up over the stitchery pattern and trace the design using a fine-tipped fabric marking pen. See General Techniques: Transferring Designs. If using an iron-on stitchery stabilizer, iron it on before starting the stitching to avoid thread shadows showing on the front of the work. Place the shiny side of the stabilizer on to the wrong side of your fabric and follow the manufacturer's instructions to bond it in place.

Working the Appliqué

two   You can do the appliqué before or after the stitchery has been completed – I do mine before. Using the templates provided and your favourite method of appliqué (see General Techniques: Appliqué Methods), apply the horse, its tail and mane and the sunflower centres. I used a fusible web method but if you prefer a needle-turn method you will need to add seam allowances to the shapes. I like to use Roxanne's Glue Baste It ™ to fix the shapes in position on the background, although you can use pins. Refer to General Techniques: Appliqué Methods. Stitch the appliqué shapes in position using a blind hem stitch and thread that matches the background fabric so it doesn't show. Press the finished appliqués, first on the wrong side and then on the right side.

three   Using a fine-tipped fabric marking pen, transfer the surface stitchery lines for the horse's eye, mouth and nose either freehand or using a light box. I used the fusible web method of appliqué to attach the wool sunflower petals.

Working the Stitchery

four   Now work the stitchery. The stitches used are: backstitch (BS), running stitch (RS), lazy daisy (LD) and French knots (FK). Code numbers are for Cosmo stranded embroidery threads but you could use DMC alternatives (see General Techniques: Embroidery Threads). Use two strands unless otherwise stated. Gently press the piece once all stitching is complete.

Key for Threads and Stitches

Cosmo 982 faded blue
Sunflower stems (BS)
Dots in sky (FK)
Birds (BS)
Flowers on grass (FK)

Cosmo 312 dark brown
Tree trunk and branches (BS)
Sunflower stems (BS)
Dashed line on hill (RS)

Cosmo 575 gold
Birds' beaks (BS)
Birds' legs (BS)

Cosmo 924 light green
Random leaves on tree (LD)
Sunflower leaves (BS)
Veins on sunflower leaves (RS)
Leaves in grass (LD)

Cosmo 895 charcoal
Horse's eye (BS)
Horse's nose (FK)
Horse's mouth (BS)
Birds' eyes (FK)

Cosmo 925 dark green
Random leaves on tree (LD)
Hill (BS)

five Make a template for the arch from template plastic (seam allowance already included). Centre the arch over your stitchery, draw around it with a fabric marking pen and cut out on the drawn line. Turn under all round by ¼in (6mm), tack (baste) and press. Stitch the stitchery centrally on the blue print background. Now sew the 1½in x 12½in (3.8cm x 31.8cm) strip of feature print to the bottom of the blue print – see Fig 1.

Fig 1

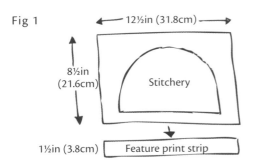

Making the Ohio Star Blocks

six To make one 3½in (8.9cm) Ohio Star Block, cut:
four 1½in (3.8cm) squares (a),
one 2¼in (5.7cm) square, recut into four triangles (b),
two 2¼in (5.7cm) squares, recut into four triangles (c),
one 2¼in (5.7cm) square, recut into four triangles (d),
one 1½in (3.8cm) square (e).

seven Using a ¼in (6mm) seam join one (c) triangle to a (b) triangle and (c) dark triangle to a (d) triangle as shown in Fig 2A. Press seams towards the dark fabric. Now join the two units together, matching up the centre seam carefully (2B). Check that the unit is 1½in (3.8cm) square trimming if not. Make three more quarter-square triangle units like this.

Fig 2

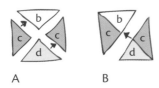

A   B

eight Take the four quarter-square triangle units, the single (e) square and the four (a) squares and arrange in the order shown in Fig 3A. Sew the units together in rows (Fig 3B) and then sew the rows together. The finished block (Fig 3C) should be 3½in (8.9cm) – check and trim if necessary. Repeat to make three more Ohio Star blocks.

Fig 3

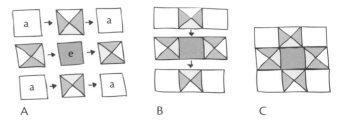

A   B   C

nine Using ¼in (6mm) seams, join the four Ohio Star blocks together (Fig 4), matching seam junctions carefully. Sew this unit to the centre block, beneath the feature print strip.

Fig 4

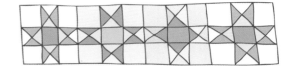

Adding the Border

ten From brown print you will need to cut:
one 18½in (47cm) square for the pillow back,
two 3½in x 8½in (8.9cm x 21.6cm) strips for side borders,
two 3½in x 18½in (8.9cm x 47cm) strips for the top and bottom borders.

Join the two shorter border strips to the sides of the centre panel as shown in Fig 5A. Press seams outwards. Now sew the two longer border strips to the centre panel and press seams (Fig 5B).

Fig 5

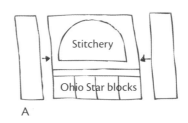

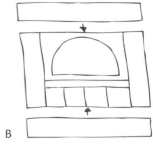

A   B

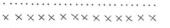 

Making Up the Pillow

eleven Following the manufacturer's instructions, bond the iron-on pellon to the wrong sides of both the pillow backing and the stitchery pillow front.

twelve Place the pillow front and back right sides together and stitch around the edge with a ¼in (6mm) seam. Leave an opening of approximately 4in (10.2cm) in what will be the bottom of the pillow, to allow you to turn the pillow to the right side and fill it with stuffing (Fig 6). Turn the pillow through to the right side, push out the corners neatly and gently press the pillow edges. Stuff the pillow and then stitch the opening closed.

Fig 6

Place right sides together and machine stitch the two layers together

Leave open here

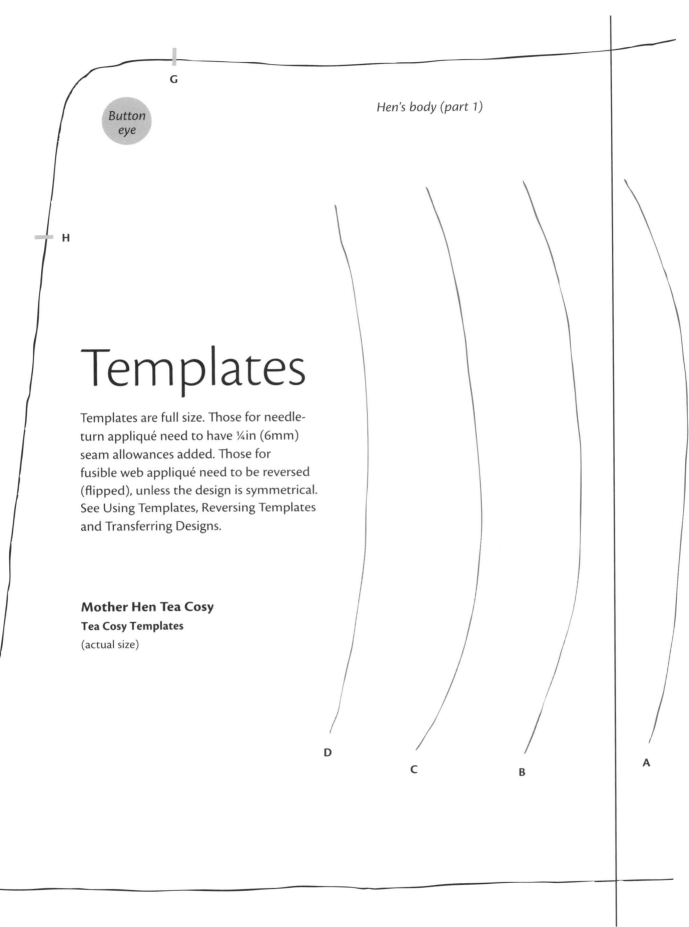

G

Button eye

Hen's body (part 1)

H

Templates

Templates are full size. Those for needle-turn appliqué need to have ¼in (6mm) seam allowances added. Those for fusible web appliqué need to be reversed (flipped), unless the design is symmetrical. See Using Templates, Reversing Templates and Transferring Designs.

Mother Hen Tea Cosy

Tea Cosy Templates

(actual size)

D

C

B

A

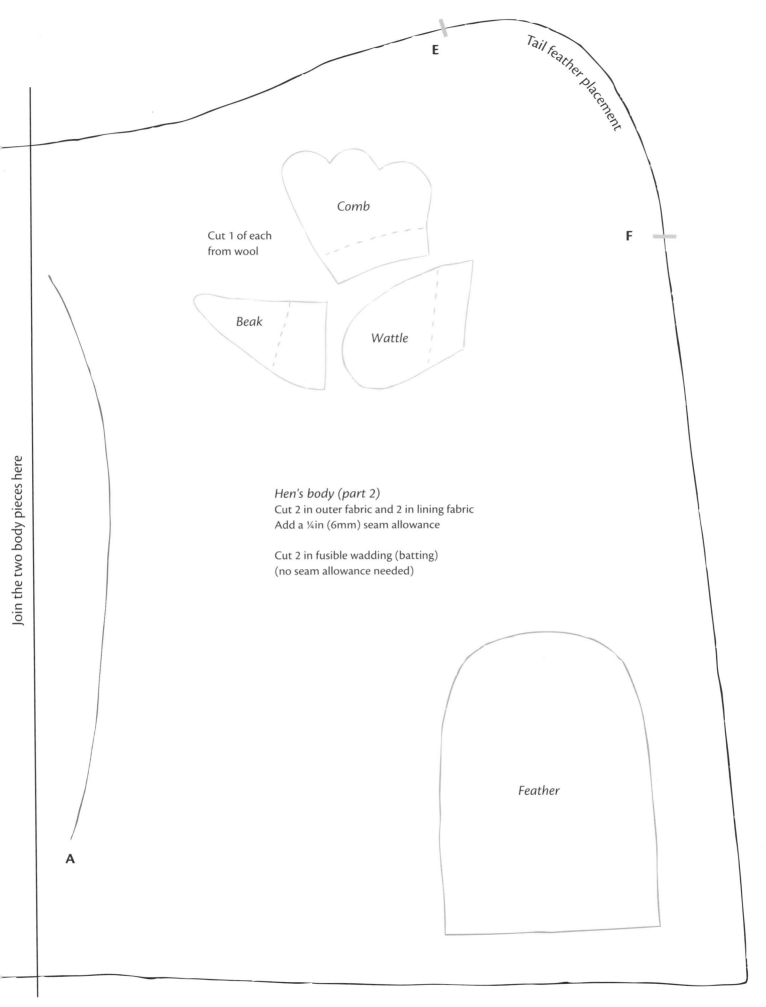

E

Tail feather placement

F

Comb

Cut 1 of each
from wool

Beak

Wattle

Join the two body pieces here

Hen's body (part 2)
Cut 2 in outer fabric and 2 in lining fabric
Add a ¼in (6mm) seam allowance

Cut 2 in fusible wadding (batting)
(no seam allowance needed)

Feather

A

Sunflower Purse
Appliqué Templates
(actual size)

Flower centre
Cut 2

Wing

Hen

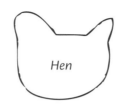

Flower
Cut 2 from wool

Add ¼in (6mm) seam allowance to the shapes if using a needle-turn appliqué method

If using fusible web appliqué the templates will need to be reversed

Hill

Sunflower Purse
Stitchery Design
(actual size)

Red lines indicate appliqué
Black lines indicate stitchery
Blue lines indicate surface stitchery

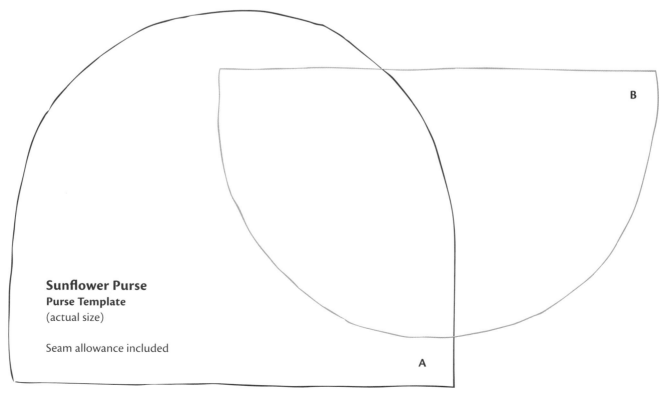

B

Sunflower Purse
Purse Template
(actual size)

Seam allowance included

A

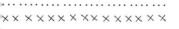 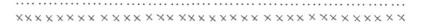

Chicken Table Centre
Appliqué Templates
(actual size)

- - - - Indicates an area that will be under another piece of appliqué

Add ¼in (6mm) seam allowance to the shapes if using a needle-turn appliqué method

If using fusible web appliqué the templates will need to be reversed

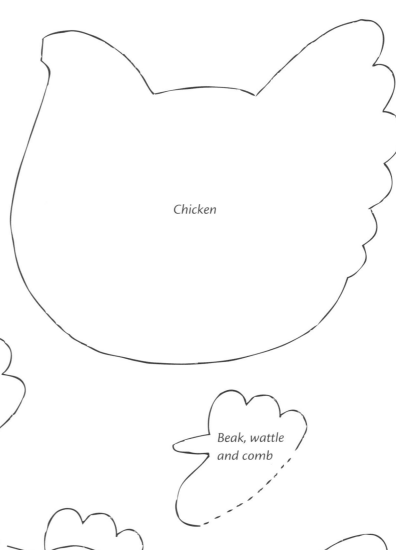

Chicken

Wing

Beak, wattle and comb

Chicken Table Centre
Appliqué placement

Button for eye

Apple Tree Farm Picture
Appliqué Templates
(actual size)

- - - - Indicates an area that will be
under another piece of appliqué

Add ¼in (6mm) seam allowance to the
shapes if using a needle-turn appliqué
method

If using fusible web appliqué the
templates will need to be reversed

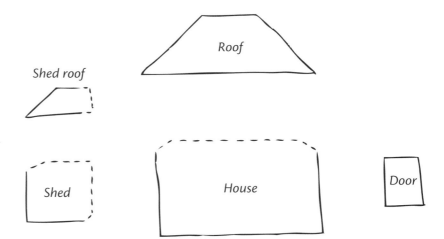

Shed roof

Roof

Shed

House

Door

Flower
Cut 2 from wool

Flower centre
Cut 2

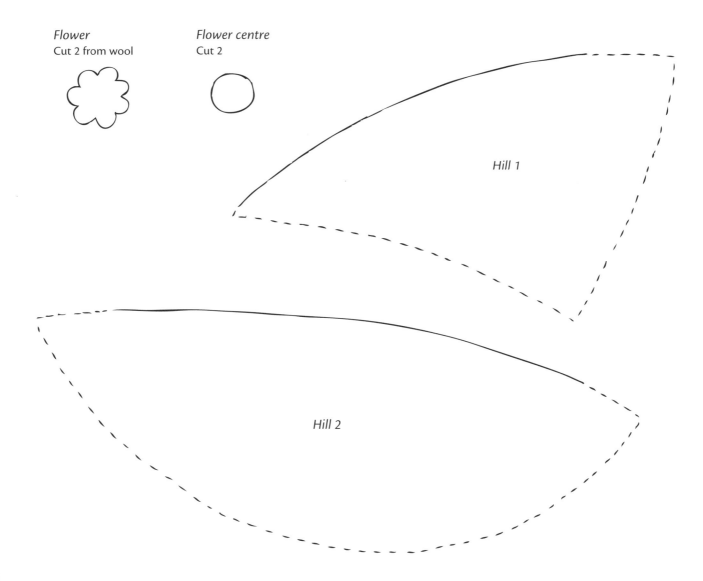

Hill 1

Hill 2

Apple Tree Farm Picture
Stitchery Design
(actual size)

Red lines indicate appliqué
Black lines indicate stitchery
Blue lines indicate surface stitchery

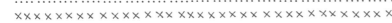

Striped Tote Bag
Hexagon Templates
(actual size)

Paper template
1½in (3.8cm) sides
Use this to cut paper templates
if you are not using pre-cut
water-soluble hexagons

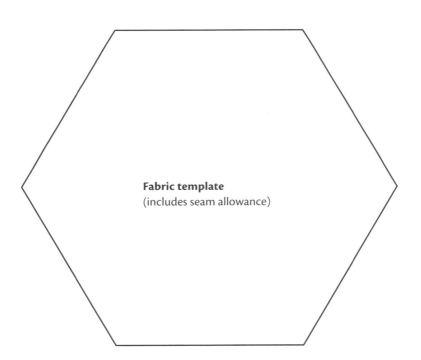

Fabric template
(includes seam allowance)

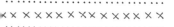 

Mrs Hen Basket

Drawing to show colour placement

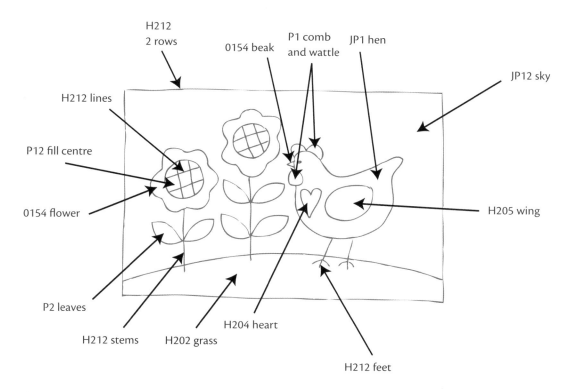

Mrs Hen Basket
Punchneedle design
(actual size)

Punchneedle design has been
reversed ready for use

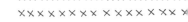

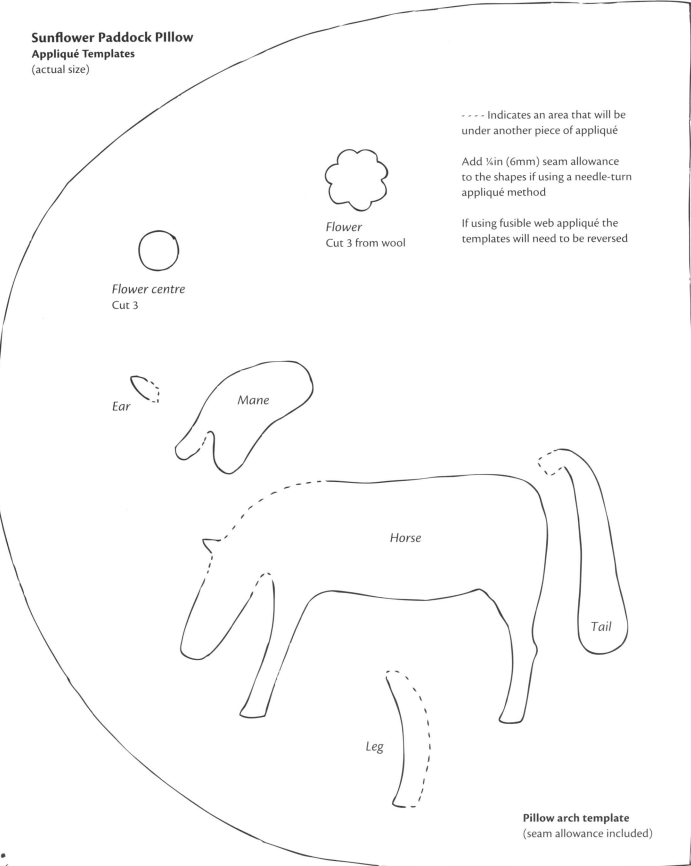

Sunflower Paddock Pillow
Appliqué Templates
(actual size)

- - - - Indicates an area that will be
under another piece of appliqué

Add ¼in (6mm) seam allowance
to the shapes if using a needle-turn
appliqué method

If using fusible web appliqué the
templates will need to be reversed

Flower
Cut 3 from wool

Flower centre
Cut 3

Ear

Mane

Horse

Tail

Leg

Pillow arch template
(seam allowance included)

44

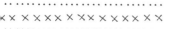
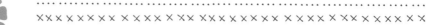

Sunflower Paddock PIllow
Stitchery Design
(actual size)

Red lines indicate appliqué
Black lines indicate stitchery
Blue lines indicate surface stitchery

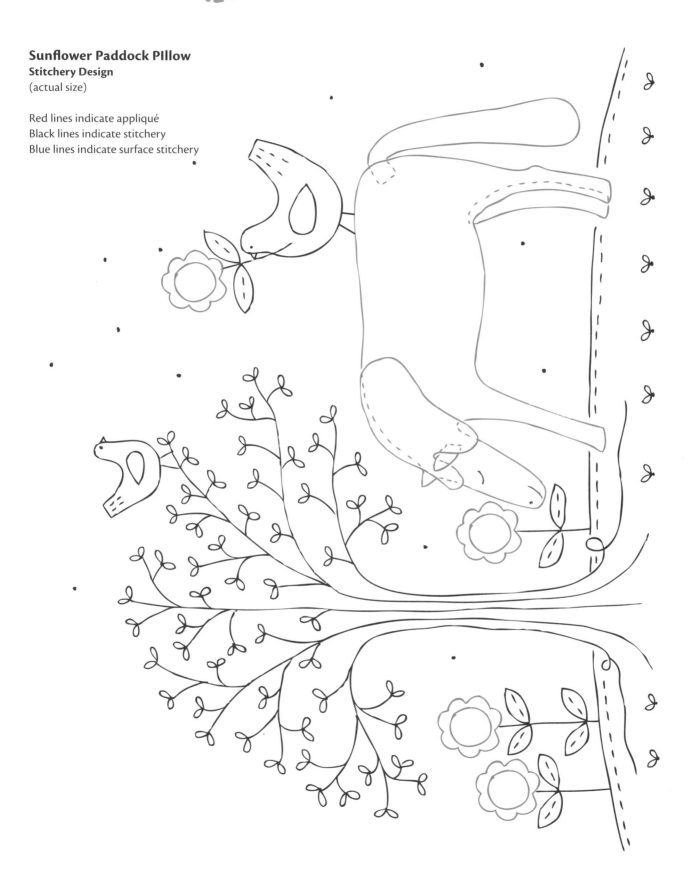

Suppliers

AUSTRALIA

Little Quilt Store
924 David Low Way, Marcoola, Sunshine
Coast, QLD 4564 Australia
T: +61 (7) 5450 7497
E: sales@littlequiltstore.com.au
www.littlequiltstore.com
*For Lynette's books, fabrics, buttons,
frames, English paper pieces, Cosmo
threads, Valdani thread, zips, bag fittings
and straps*

Lynette Anderson Designs
PO Box 9314, Pacific Paradise, QLD 4564
Australia
T: +61 (7) 5450 7497
E: info@lynetteandersondesigns.com.au
www. lynetteandersondesigns.com.au
Wholesale enquires and teaching info

Moss Recycled Vintage Handcrafted Furniture Steptoes of Coolum
132, Greenoaks Drive, Coolum Beach ,
Queensland 4573 Australia

French and Gorgeous
Shop 13, Peregain Shopping Village, 12
Grebe Street, Peregian Beach, QLD 4573
Australia
T: +61 7 5471 2936

Sandra Faye Photographer
www.sandrafayephotographer.com.au

CANADA

Chicken Feed Quilts
1401 20 Ave Coaldale, Alberta T1M 1A2
T: +1 (403) 345-4048
E: hipchick@chickenfeedquilts.com
For Lynette's books, fabrics and buttons

UK & EUROPE

Stitch Craft Create
Brunel House, Forde Close,
Newton Abbot, Devon, TQ12 4PU
www.stitchcraftcreate.co.uk

Cotton and Color
Inzlingerstrasse 279, 4125 Riehen, 1,
Swittzerland
T: +41(0)616413770
www.info@cotton-color.com

Cross Patch
Blaen Bran Farm, Velindre, Llandysul,
Carmarthenshire SA44 5XT
T: +44 01559 371018
E: enquiries@cross-patch.co.uk
For Lynette's books, fabrics and buttons

USA

The Rabbits Lair
116 West Walnut Street, Rogers AR 72756
T: +1 479 636 3385
E: info@therabbitslair.com
For Lynette's books, fabrics and buttons

Jo-Ann Stores Inc
5555 Darrow Road, Hudson, Ohio, USA
T: 1 888 739 4120
E: guest service@jo-annstores.com
www.joann.com
*Mail order and shops – for craft,
needlework and quilting supplies, including
weaver's cloth and Cameo Ultra Punch tool*

Martha Pullen
149 Old Big Cove Road
Brownsboro, AL 35741
www.marthapullen.com

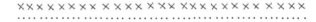

Index

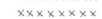

About the Author

Lynette Anderson's love affair with textiles began at a young age when she was growing up in a small village in Dorset, England, where her grandmother taught her to embroider and knit. Patchwork caught Lynette's attention in 1981 after the birth of her first son, and her affinity with textiles is apparent in her work. Moving with her family to Australia in 1990 prompted the release of Lynette first patterns in 1995 and over the years Lynette has produced hundreds of patterns. Her distinctive yet sophisticated naïve design style encompasses quilts, pillow, bags and sewing accessories. Lynette also designs wooden buttons, which are cut to her original drawings and hand-painted locally to her specifications. Each year Lynette designs a wonderful quilt for button club members using her unique buttons.

In 2010 Lynette was very excited to be able to fulfil her dream of putting her designs on to fabric when she was asked to design for Lecien Fabrics. Collections include 'Summertime Friends', 'Scandinavian Christmas', 'Secret Garden', 'Hollyhock Cottage', 'Happy Halloween', 'Christmas Fun' and 'Follow My Heart'. A busy year is planned for 2013 with the release of fabric collections called 'Wildflower Wood', 'Candy Cane Angels' and 'Mending Fences'.

Lynette's first professionally published book, *It's Quilting Cats & Dogs*, was for David & Charles in 2010 and is filled with heart-warming designs that combine simple but stunning hand stitchery with traditional patchwork and quilting. This was followed by *Country Cottage Quilts* in March 2012, with a lovely collection of projects showcasing Lynette's original and distinctive style. A charming collection of festive designs, *Stitch It For Christmas*, was published in 2012 and *Stitch It For Spring* in May 2013.

For more about Lynette visit her blog: www.lynetteandersondesigns.typepad.com

Acknowledgments

I am blessed with having so many people willing to help with the many tasks that need to be done to create the projects for a book like this. Firstly, I would like to thank Emma and Lyn, who work tirelessly in the office giving me the time I need to draw, stitch and create. Thanks to Val Tanner, who does the loveliest embroidery and who is always willing to help. 'Ginger' the hen – her feathers never ruffled once, even though we asked her to hold her pose while the ever-patient Sandra took photos. To Lea, Von and Helen, who all have wonderful stores filled with fabulous vintage furniture, thank you for the loan of all the vintage and recycled props that we used throughout the book.

A DAVID & CHARLES BOOK
© F&W Media International, Ltd 2013

David & Charles is an imprint of F&W Media
International, Ltd
Brunel House, Forde Close, Newton Abbot,
TQ12 4PU, UK

F&W Media International, Ltd is a subsidiary of
F+W Media, Inc
10151 Carver Road, Suite #200, Blue Ash,
OH 45242, USA

Text and Designs © Lynette Anderson 2013
Layout and Photography © F&W Media
International, Ltd 2013

First published in the UK and USA in 2013

Lynette Anderson has asserted her right to be
identified as author of this work in accordance
with the Copyright, Designs and Patents Act, 1988.

A catalogue record for this book is available from
the British Library.

ISBN-13: 978-1-4463-0319-1 paperback
ISBN-10: 1-4463-0319-5 paperback

Printed in China by RR Donnelley for:
F&W Media International, Ltd
Brunel House, Forde Close, Newton Abbot,
TQ12 4PU, UK

10 9 8 7 6 5 4 3 2 1

Acquisitions Editor: Sarah Callard
Desk Editor: Matthew Hutchings
Project Editor: Linda Clements
Designer: Jennifer Stanley
Photographer: Sandra Faye
Production Controller: Kelly Smith

F+W Media publishes high quality books on
a wide range of subjects.
For more great book ideas visit:
www.stitchcraftcreate.co.uk